Healing of the Heart

Healing of the Heart

Lessons From My Journey

KEISHA D. HENRY

Contents

Introduction

Life is a journey of diverse destinations. I think some people, for the most part, try to plan their lives, with a definite purpose in mind. However, if you are like me, the word "plan" was very from your vocabulary, much less your vision. Truthfully, "dense fog" was more like it for me!

My mother immigrated to the United States when I was seven years old. I felt lost in this new and strange environment. Making matters worse, the turbulent period of adolescence was exacerbated due to the absence of my father. My mother was a single mom, and life was difficult.

Life yields results depending on which side of the tracks you're born, the family you are born in, your socio-economic environment and, among others, your effort. Whatever we are harvesting now in our lives is a result of what was planted many yesterday's ago.

The planting of seeds by ourselves and others invariably yields destinations, "a harvest" that's unpleasant and disappointing. Sometimes they reinforce untruths about ourselves, and thereby create false identity.

What can we do with this non-preferred "harvest?" "Healing of the Heart," poetry and journal book, is exactly what came out of mine. Healing of the Heart is a guided poetry journal to help you navigate the humps and ditches impacting your "destination" and "harvest" – the one you choose this time.

Understanding that vulnerability is necessary for healing of self and others, I have been transparent in sharing some critical moments in my life. Out of the years of "dense fog" I have discovered a lifechanging formula, enabling me to overcome fear and unbelief. This formula has been useful in helping me and many women and girls whom I have been privileged to work with.

Why not rewrite your story? Why not plant creative seeds so you can reap a harvest that is authentic and fulfilling. You can change your destiny by changing your mind. Purpose awaits you. Go meet and fulfill it!

Intro: Faith

It is so hard to leave the past behind: people who have robbed us and difficult circumstances or environments. Maybe even people whom you and I have in turn caused harm. It can be difficult to live in an abundance mindset, especially if "lack" was conditioned and promoted early in life and for a long time.

If we are not "mindful" we replicate the same behaviours or the same environments due to pre-conditioning. When difficulty arises, we respond from the old self (lack mindset) rather than by the new inherited constitution, received upon conversion.

"Lack" thoughts, feelings and behaviours undermine wellbeing and power. Among others, they manifest as people pleasing, dependency on others, sadness, loneliness and uncertainty. Honestly, these are the ones that come for me. Since the mind can be conditioned and controlled, I have decided to do so by faith – belief. I have decided to leave the past behind, leave other people behind, leave negative "suggestions and narratives" about me behind. How? By cultivating and practicing faith. I do so by renewing my mind with truths daily.

I had to develop self-confidence and a better way of thinking about myself and life. This practice I have now called the "My Belief Formula." I have developed it out of desperation to be whole. It worked! I have used it with other women and girls in my work. They report success with it. This is a lifetime of practice. I have provided a copy for you in the back of this journal. Start today!

Be not conformed to the pattern of this world; but be ye transformed by the renewing of your mind.

— ROMANS 12:2 —

Faith

Feeling lonely but confident,
Sad but holding to faith.
Doubt wants to creep in but belief is speaking,
Reminding that Jesus is whom I'm trusting.

Yet doubt is everywhere like sand,
When it gets in your shoes and refuses to move.
The more you shake, the more it appears and settles,
Questioning pluck and mettle.

The only solution is to wash with water.
That's what faith is to doubt.
The water of the Word
Removes the dark clouds and keeps me faithful.

There's good tidings, peace and laughter…
Faith is restoring and removing disaster.
The stealer of life shall not have its way.
It must surrender to Life-Giver and Master.

Intro: Elevate Me

"I believe I am lovable." "I believe I am worthy." These words are so difficult to say out loud and to believe. They sound fake. Yet they are honest reflections of myself and many women and girls that I have talked with.

Unfortunately, negative conditioning has made it difficult to accept and say out loud even what I know to be true, and has made it difficult to develop my spiritual relationship. I felt like I could not go to God and openly express myself. He would not understand, or care to listen, or care about my pain.

Negative self-talk came from early childhood experiences. They created negative thought-patterns steeped in fear and doubt. Sadly, these experiences came from well-meaning people, who said they were "Christians" or "spiritual" – people that spoke to the same God to whom I hoped to speak. I thought, "Why should I talk to the "God" to whom those well-meaning persons spoke. Besides, these people were misguided and caused harm.

Inner conflicts caused the hiding of my pain for many years. One day, I became desperate! I had often been asked whether religion, belief in God or spirituality made any difference. My prayer life was challenged. Like me, people questioned whether there was any real efficacy in prayer and whether it mattered if prayers were said quietly or loudly.

I discovered God really answered prayers and that posture and volume didn't matter. Connection with God, faith, motive, sincerity and earnestness were some of the things that counted. Practice, belief in prayer and faith in God allowed me to experience true love and acceptance of myself. Despite the fact, broken ways sometimes try to return, wanting me to "forget to remember." The practice of prayer

and belief can elevate the mind, will and emotions. I know this to be
true for God has continued to elevate me in so many ways.

I praise you (God) because I am fearfully and
wonderfully made; your (His) works are wonderful.
I know that full well.

Prompt: What do I currently believe about God? How have my
thoughts about God as Father influenced by my experiences with my
own father or mother?

Elevate Me

Lord elevate me from this place.
This place of doubt, pain, and anger;
So I can feel your presence and be stronger

Lord elevate me from this place
Of fear and loneliness—to see your face
And at your feet your tender mercies embrace.

Lord elevate me from this place.
Call me to come where you reside
Where there's peace and rest whatever betide.

Lord elevate me from this place.
My soul is weary and my heart is faint
I need you now to lift the weight.

Lord elevate me from this place.
He did come—but I did not stay.
I wondered from the narrow way.
I forgot to remember.

Intro: Living in Their Shadow

After accomplishing so much in the last year, I still woke up feeling uncertain about myself and many things. I reflected on the work that I did: starting and sustaining a blog, writing for 3 magazines and supporting the lives of other women. I still did not feel accomplished, like I was not enough. This feeling is not new. It has been gnawing at me from the very beginning, since I realized that I was a person.

This old feeling swept me away. I began to look up a friend of mine, online, that went to law school. She had actually mentored me to get in. I went online and looked her up and saw her accomplishments and started to feel horrible about not completing law school. As I am writing, I began to see that I was diminishing my adversity, dishonouring myself, minimizing my courage in the face of struggles, my path and my purpose.

I came to see that the experience I'm so ashamed of was allowed by God to prepare me for what He had prepared for me. Adversity was a test and preparation. I grew up hearing and was told as early as the age of 3 that I was to be a lawyer. I can tell you, I never felt that in my heart. I did not. What I felt was turmoil, uncertainty and a desire to figure out who I was; a desire to feel whole and like I mattered. You guessed it: I did not finish law school.

To be a lawyer was not the plan birthed in my heart. God had another plan for me. As I grew older and began working on my soul (mind, emotions and will) I realize that I did not have a passion for law—just the status and title to please those who said that was what I needed to be.

Two years ago, I finally felt peace about the matter. I showed my daughters, Kira and Elizabeth, my transcripts wherein I needed .5 to pass that semester and I failed. Yes, after completing college in 3 years, in a hurry to get to law school and sitting the LSAT twice, this was the outcome. I looked at the transcript with tears, mourning the need to be someone that mattered.

— ROMANS 14:22 —

Prompt: What was born in your heart that you still have yet to honour?

Living In Their Shadow

Despite past failures, pain and suffering
You're a person of worth,
A child of the King.

Valuable creature you are,
Destined to light the earth,
Like sun, moon and star.

There's a plan for your life
You have dreams and beliefs.
Hope is waiting to take flight

Come up higher!
What are you doing down there?
Forget naysayers and relinquish fears

A seat at the table for you is set,
Up-front and Center.
Don't you ever forget.

Understand who you are…
Fear is a reproach… not a truth teller.
You're a woman of valor, purpose, and honour.

"Your gifts will make room for you"… I'm told.
Be a good steward and not a squanderer.
Then I understood…

Who says you have to do
And say what they like?
Grab the mic.

The platform is yours…
It's time to make your move
Move with rhythm and gait.

It's your choice now, maybe not back then…
Don't leave it up to them!
Move with confidence and try again.

Intro: Begin Again

This stuff can show up in your marriage and parenting relationships – things like poor self-esteem, unresolved issues and insecurities – baggage from the past, including parent-child relationships. Baggage weighed me down. Due to baggage, I found myself responding instead of listening: always "defending" instead of connecting emotionally, essentially making "everything about me" and from a negative place of being.

Connecting emotionally is a deficit I've had for a long time. I have had to work hard to grow through this for the sake of my family, especially my children. Oh! The blunders that came before. In the midst of trying to meet the needs of those depending on me, I was in conflict trying to meet my own needs, because I often felt misunderstood and judged.

At times I wanted to retreat to protect myself. Thankfully, some encounters were different. These exceptions were my children, spouse and mentors. They were compassionate enough, which encouraged me to take a better look at myself. From them, I learned to examine myself without judgment, to be compassionate to myself and begin again.

My mentor, Sharon Cohan, always said, "Your life experiences will prove valuable to your clients one day." In other words, there's no need to be ashamed of your life; begin again. Yet here I was, thinking I had to be perfect!

Prompt: Have the seeds of discouragement planted from childhood echoed in your adult life? How about viewing the echo as an opportunity to relearn?

Begin Again

Begin again… It's time sufficient.
Every thought, every second counts…
There's no problem you can't surmount.

What you plant will truly grow…
So be intentional about what you sow.
Sow seeds of hope, belief and determination.

Weeds will bring discouragement and doubt,
And obstruct your aspiration.
Be prepared and be a good scout.

Do not let discouragement count you out.
Time to put your dreams into action.
Success requires persistent and calculated motion.

There has to be devotion and perspiration.
Begin again… it's the only way to win.
When life is hitting back, launch your own attack!

No need to retreat or surrender!
With desire, faith and a sound plan
What or whom can withstand?

Intro: He Did Do It

I did not know that a broken person is conspicuous to the naked eye. Be that as it may, it is certainly possible spiritually. I remember being a pregnant at 17 ½ years old. Close to my 18th birthday, a woman said these words to me: "God is going to use you and give you a ministry out of this." The woman, Sherma Maynard, from Trinidad & Tobago, was the guest speaker, who spoke prophetically over my life. This was at a church convention.

Emotions ran high during this encounter and at that period of time. I was definitely a skeptic regarding her statement and felt that I was a disappointment to God, myself and many others. I felt like "Yeah, you have now become part of the statistic in America." I thought I was done for! Dense fog really was amplified at this period. I truly had no vision for myself. So, how could God use me – for what and when?

Those words at the women's church conference came back to me forcefully at the end of our New Beginning Healing Institute's Women Self-Esteem & Self-Improvement Group on December 16, 2021. While cleaning up the room tears flooded my face as I recalled my position then and what is now.

If that was not enough proof of God's love and providence or if you are a skeptic about purpose, consider this next exchange: In December, 2021, I was visiting a place that I frequented. A woman and her husband whom I had seen on a couple occasions were there. On this encounter, she declared: "You are an instrument for other women and God will use you to help them, given your own past trials and tribulations." Please note that I do not know or have ever exchanged a word with her or her husband.

Now therefore thus saith the Lord of hosts; consider your ways.

— Haggai 1:5 —

Prompt: What negative conclusions do you still hold about yourself? How does your spirituality help or impede you? What do you think you should do about it?

He Did Do It!

From my pain has come purpose.
It happened right before my eyes.
No magic, no, not even a circus.
A divine plan from the omniscient one!
Many detours,
Strong winds, inclement weather...
I did not know I would make it...
But He knew better.
Self-hate and fear my name and person did bear...
Shame and doubt had me muzzled—trying to dictate...
As if I have no say about my destiny, my future...
But now, here's my testimony
I am "The Madam Chair"
My life, my dreams, my hopes
You are now spectators...
No longer my antagonists or masters...
Setting up divisions of who is first and who is last...
You get to sit in silence and give counsel ONLY when asked.
I did it you see!
I did it!
Right before your eyes...
No magic, no, not even a circus...
From my pain has come my purpose...
A divine plan from the omniscient one!
He did it... I did it. We did it.

Intro: Know Your Worth

It's so easy to blame, especially when we feel hurt or have been hurt by others. Between 5 and 8 years-of-age, my mom or grandmother would dress me up. Why? For the big day – to see dad. I would wait for hours on end for him to arrive from Kingston, to see me in Montego-Bay, where I lived at the time. Dad was a tall, handsome and stately policeman.

I admired him and wanted to be the "apple of his eye." Guess what? My father never came! This happened on several occasions – dressing up, my twin brother and I, only to hear "Oh! he probably had to stop along the way for police stuff and got tied up." This was the beginning of "feelings of abandonment."

To feel unloved and abandoned by a significant other is distressing, to say the least. These negative emotions can set you up to fail in life. My future was marred and contaminated by these experiences. Why? They impacted how I felt about myself and had a negative impact on my relationships. Research has shown that between ages 5-7 a child's belief system is cemented—hardened!

I know what it's like to not feel a father's love. I know what it's like to lack confidence in myself and to be uncertain of my identity. It became easy to blame myself for things, become a people pleaser or doormat to gain the affection of others, and to ultimately blame others when things do not turn out the way I had hoped.

Along the way, I realized I had a decision to make! I had to repair my belief system – do an overhaul! I am an adult now, and responsible for my decisions and future. I decided to cultivate and realize my worth. Here is a quote that has helped me. I hope it will help you as well and motivate intentional growth:

No sense in passing judgment on the past.
No one has been unambiguously right or wrong.
It's the collective experience that matters.

— Sir Derek Walcott —

Prompt: What are the stories that happened between the ages of 5-7 that shaped your belief system? And, what part or parts of your belief system needs to be repaired for you to fully realize your worth?

Begin Your Belief Repair Affirmation:

I AM CREATED GOOD
I AM CREATED WHOLE
I AM CREATED LOVED

Know Your Worth

You made it seem like something was wrong with me…
My request or simple girl nuances dismissed,
So I second-guessed.
On birthdays no cards… You made it seem hard
Unimportant, trivial, these actions became a sequel.

All along I was not your intended… only your gain,
And whatever you could have extracted…
After a while, my eyes opened in denial still refusing to accept.
How could this be?

The many inconveniences you have dealt.
The many disregards and discards my heart has felt.
Then suddenly my eyes, heart, and soul finally accepted.

I am good, whole and loved.
These you desire and can only dream of.
You are empty, producing only weeds and moss.
To mar and destroy others is your loss

Intro: Nature Speaks

I had just transitioned to a new administrative position. A promotion! My father died a few months into the transition. Life changed forever. I found myself in a work position and environment that felt so familiar. I felt unsupported and observed cliques and double-standards.

Ultimately, I felt psychologically and emotionally unsafe. I went into protective mode. The days, weeks and months ahead there felt like "deja vu," like I had been here before. There was no one to turn to. Everyone seemed timid to say how they felt about anything. And there was no room for me to be myself. The environment was toxic! I faced isolation, intimidation and loneliness.

The old adage, "Do as I say, not as I do" was the modus operandi. I could not understand how a decision to grow turned into a disaster, I thought. Tears became my meal morning and night, literally. I wondered why God abandoned me. Worse yet, there was doubleabandonment: I felt, my dad with whom I was beginning to salvage a relationship, having past.

A few days after dad passed, while meditating I discovered that what I thought was a derailment was actually an alignment. I saw the gift his death provided. The gift of moving on without him and becoming what I am to be. I saw the gift of the hardship in the administrative position as preparation for the future. Now, here I am! Ultimately, *Christ was in everything.* He did not miss a beat. He truly goes at his own pace: nature shows this. I am learning to harmonize with nature and with Him.

I give you this to take with you nothing remains as it was.
If you know this, you can begin again with joy in the uprooting.

— Judith Minty —

Prompt: Spending time observing nature helps reduce depression and anxiety. Practice spending time observing nature and journal how you feel when finished.

23

Nature Speaks

The sun rises and sets.
Even the ocean ebbs and flows.
A natural reset.
Trees have roots, trunks, and leaves.
They function by their foundation.

My existence, too, requires each of these steps,
Foundation integral to my evolution.
My being, heart, soul, and spirit
is also His creation…
Yet I suffer without his renewing.

Now my walks are no longer lonely
Every path guided…
My entrance and access granted…
Exits divinely orchestrated.

Thoughts and imagination lifted and elevated.
Solipsism, sovereignty is my consciousness…
Awareness, summer or spring,
He's in everything
Winter or Fall, I count it all joy!

Intro: The Narcissist

We are all born narcissists, at least to some extent. Why? We are all born with needs. These needs are to be met by a nurturing mother and father. If not, we grow into persons who seek to have those infantile needs met at any cost, even at the expense of our self-worth. I know about this quite well.

There are many things denied us physically, spiritually, emotionally and intellectually, for one reason or another. The consequent turbulence has impaired some for life. Caregivers either could not do better or tended to their own survival needs.

As we age, we may encounter narcissism in friends, colleagues, partners or spouses. After years of wanting to feel important, understood, loved and wanted, we easily attract people who are narcissist, essentially people looking to have their needs met too. In such a scenario, a collision course is definite!

Narcissists take without mercy – emotionally, spiritually and financially, and can leave a person bankrupt. Sometimes they "swoop in" with much charm, only to leave one "high and dry." Without realizing what is happening, a person may be found on a "rollercoaster" of a relationship, consisting of the same elements and outcomes. What's done is never enough, leaving victims feeling robbed, abused and confused, reinforcing childhood traumas. This has been my experience and that of many women.

It's hard to realize one's worth or self-esteem after these experiences with narcissistic partners and even parents. At some point, you and I have to determine when "enough is enough." Time enough to begin to heal and meet our emotional needs.

It took me to realize my gift. I am my gift.

— Yvonne Orji —

Prompt: 5 questions to help build resilience and meet emotional needs.

- What perspective or view do you have that needs changing?

- Where or whom do you need to start saying no to?

- In what ways can you show kindness to yourself?

- What interests and hobbies do you have or need to cultivate?

- In what ways do you need to manage your time and emotional energy?

To The Narcissist

Such a waste of time taking up my mind,
Taking up so much space in my heart and head,
Always want to take and not give.
Is that the way you plan to live?
Far be it from me…
I have a choice you see.
Your unrelenting desire is clear
You give off smoke
To distract from the evidence
That has always been there.
What are you?
Who are you?
Two faces… underneath a dark bottomless pit,
A person empty and cold
Pretending be confident and certain.
Yet actually waiting to be freed.
You have snared and spoiled many.
"Just one more… just one more," you tell yourself,
Only to remain in the same prison
Of selfishness, jealousy and shame.
Yet you're unwilling to change and free yourself.

Intro: The Unknown

I know all too well what it is like to have no sense of self and to not be goal-oriented. This can be crippling! And it was for a long time. In those moments, I replayed "tapes of old thoughts." Yes, I continued to self-fulfil what was told me by others and by my negative experiences. Pistons fired together were wired together, basically reinforcing old emotions and old pathways in my brain.

I remember saying to myself, "What good can come from me?" It's one thing to have superficial unbelief, like most intelligent people. This was clearly not me. I tried to have solid dreams and plans. However, my mind, emotions and will were compromised; and my essence toxic.

Admittedly, I had little belief in my abilities – or even knew what they were. My brain could not complete a picture. This meant not seeing things through that I started and at best being mediocre. At some point, I began to question myself about my own predicament. This allowed me to create unknown.

It's ok for me to be myself, vulnerable and without judgment.

— K. Henry —

Prompt: In what ways are you still waiting to be told that you are great? Upon discovery, now ask yourself what you feel should be done about it?

The Unknown

Creating the unknown takes courage,
I have to be bold.
Often I limit myself by what I already know.
I don't know sometimes—most times where I'm going.
I just know I have to keep rowing.
The tides of life, seemingly insurmountably high.
The signs are not always clear.
My emotions are everywhere – reeling with fear underneath.
There's something I want and feel very strongly about
But there're moments when I'm filled with doubt.
My heart pounds.
Questions fall like rain—not like a thunderstorm,
The one that goes on and on…
Then I realize there's purpose in the storm:
Water—a refilling of the seas and estuaries,
Flowing to unknown places and sanctuaries,
Satisfying yet disrupting collective stasis.
Opportunities, moments, straight paths,
Unexpected detours unknown known before
Reminded I am still the author.
Like a lightning bolt quickening to action,
Awakening my fretful stupor.
From pasture to pasture.
Destiny may have a part or take a certain posture…

But a bystander I cannot and will not be.
An open landscape is there to seize for me.
A plain canvas screams!
Create unknowns unique to me.

Intro: Broken Not Buried

Where were you when your heart was first broken? "I seek a new heart," I remember thinking after that moment. Feeling disoriented, shocked and disappointed, I felt crippled for days, weeks, months and years to come.

Interesting how emotional wounds can have such a strong impact on one's life. Coupled with lack of self-love, emotional wounds can be devastating. I had learned to dismiss and ignore my own thoughts and feelings, and thus became dependent on others for validation. The repercussions were:

- Poor self-esteem

- Unplanned pregnancy and unwanted parenthood

- Becoming a teen Mom

- Inability to vet others

- Inability to set boundaries

- Depression

As I reflected, I was deeply disappointed with myself. In attempting to fill the void for love and unmet needs, I often fell prey to "people pleasing" in relationships and simple transactions. I allowed people to choose me rather than me choosing them. Somehow, their choice of me made me feel special, in some way. The void deepened, as long as I depended on others for validation or to meet my needs. "Foreclosure" on identity and personhood in my formative years had shaped understanding of self and relationships.

Involuntarily "foreclosure" on my life as a child, did not give me the opportunity to explore in safety with caregivers. Why? They themselves were absent for some of the same reasons. There were no distinctive, enduring patterns of a father's love. I was still seeking in others what I did not have and they could not give what they themselves had not received. In my recovery and healing, I decided this is an extreme I will not accept.

"You are created good, you are created whole,
and you are created loved."

— Keisha Henry —

Broken Not Buried

There is a clearing that is coming.
The atmosphere is changing.
Your voice I can hear.
My heart is filled with good cheer.

The valleys almost now distant.
The mountain top is on the horizon.
My eyes widen, my feet hasten.
The toil, the pain wasn't for nothing.

Discouragement came and laughed in my face.
Doubt made its boast with a daggered snout.
Fear held me hostage in every which way.
Exasperated—my faith is not as strong as I decided

HE never left—my expectations He far exceeded.
His promises I almost forfeited.
They're mine to have…
This is the grace He provided.

Intro: Paradox of Healing

Desires vs. obstacles: What can seem like a derailment or position of being stuck can be disguised as "The Purpose" – the balm, the healing for you and others. Realization and understanding can be missed – worse yet, not attended to at all. You see, an identity crisis or an unwholesome view of self can lead to a drain of emotional energy and associated consequences.

Consequences may include: lack of confidence, feelings of inadequacies and being highly dependent on others. In summary, derailment can lead to timidity, fear of challenges and changes, being risk averse, impounding desires, and failure to give birth to dreams and aspirations.

I remember the summer of 2021 when my heart was pricked to make the women's group free to the public – to any woman who wanted to change their life and heal. I remember thinking, "No one will take me seriously. Oh, they will think I am crazy or desperate." Then I thought, "Will I be able to be authentic to the women who will come?" The old, insecure part of what was given or developed in me tried to return.

The women did come! As the week progressed, the openness and willingness of the women opened up other possibilities and realizations in my own life. Had I listened to those old tapes, which emerged from the old house, I would've missed it.

My desire must equal or exceed the obstacles
I face to achieve the results I seek.

— K. Henry —

Prompt: What is it that you have to give but allowed fear to keep you locked inside?

Paradox of Healing

Giving opens feelings of healing..
Of hope beyond human ceiling.
Removes barriers that once kept you shuttered.

Shuttered like an isolated house left for ruin;
Or like that little girl inside locked in her room,
Feeling unsafe about her space in the world.

No one comes in and there's nothing going out.
The elements of life escape none
And there is no round-about.

There is no guarantee.
It is up to us to bargain and see what can
Become of our efforts, our faith, our love.

What are we really about?
So many people take and not give,
Missing the mark. This is the path they live.

Forgetting that they too, soon will cease to exist.
The purpose they missed…
"Giving is receiving" – not a myth

When we give we allow ourselves to be open
to the possibilities in the making,
The ones that giving is creating.

Anything else is dismal; nothing is growing.
Don't be deceived, giving is receiving.
This is the paradox of healing.

Intro: True Healing Is Not Blaming

Do you desire to be whole or healed? I was 23 years old when my world came tumbling down. I had failed law school and in a relationship that felt like a "parent-child relationship." So, there was no help there.

One morning, filled with anger and hurt, I somehow found my father's phone number. He lived in Kingston, Jamaica. I blamed him for EVERYTHING! Up until that moment, I held it in. You see, I had this conflicting image about my dad. I wanted to believe he was perfect and could do nothing wrong: some strange thing happened that kept him away.

Unfortunately, narratives of aunts and grandparents caused confusion and added to my dilemma – narratives about my conception and reasons why he was not around. I remember thinking "If that's who he is, then what does that make me?" "Is that why I felt like I never belonged?" "Is that why I am failing in life?"

I remember calling and letting him have it. After the call I felt worse, like a deep burning in my chest. Worse yet, nothing really changed. In a strange way, I said to myself "I may not have been his option, but I can choose me." From there on, I was no longer a victim. I became an overcomer. I chose me.

> *Do you want to be made well? The sick man answered Him,*
> *'Sir, I have no man to put me into the pool when the water is*
> *stirred up; but while I am coming, other steps down before me.'*

— John 5:7 —

Prompt: Did you know yourself before you were born? What did you learn from others about who you are?

True Healing Is Not Blaming

In one way or another, we all need healing,
A journey we must take to grow or to be well.
No point in blaming or shaming.
It's not what's done.
It's how we overcome.

We blame others or circumstances
For handicaps present and future.
So it is with many.
We define ourselves in relationship to problems
And in comparison to others.

Forfeiting powers, talents and gifts,
Mourning only and going adrift.
Overlooking the present and real treasures,
Forgetting this moment is really ours…
What then?…

We consecrate the temporary.
Quiet the mind so we can hear within
Things are always changing.
Notice the ocean with its capacity for renewing.
True healing is not blaming.

Intro: Lack of Intent

"I can see why I felt I needed you," I thought out loud while lying on the couch. It made me feel powerful and confident – like I mattered.

Needing validation is an emptiness that pops up especially when I'm taking on new projects that scare me. Unsure of myself, I feel like I don't know what I am doing or have the skills. I remember these feelings of being scared, unsure and vulnerable as a child. I finally made the connection from my adolescent years of not having dad around and saw how it affected early adulthood and beyond. I understood the unhealthy relationships I endured: they provided a false sense of security. You get a rush of power as if on drugs, which I accepted as normal. From these experiences, I realized I never had a real, pure knowledge of a father, a protector, a guide: a father and daughter love relationship. So, the unhealthy, toxic, impure form of love was craved, which was painful at times. This impostor misled and disappointed.

Dad not being there was not surprising: there was no intent. The void he left, though, damaged personhood and self-esteem. As a result, people and circumstances exploited me. I was vulnerable.

Now that I know better, I can assert myself and make better choices. My life is not theirs; it's mine. God has given free will. With his guidance, I have learned to cultivate and practice that which is good and wholesome.

Meditating and writing this poem has made me realized that I am enough. In a strange way, my soul is finally whole—the mystery is complete. I am no longer a puzzle of broken pieces. This search, this longing and constant questioning is over.

Prompt: What negative truths about you have shaped your life, socially and emotionally?

Lack of Intent

Lack of intent…
Is the same "one" that tried to follow me
Into adulthood… the people I chose
Or allowed to choose me

The hole that desperately needed to be filled
Became deeper and wider,
Almost like a crater.
So has been my journey

On a course without wander,
I witnessed moves which caused me to ponder.
There were many questions but no answers.
I felt like an unskilled rider on a wild horse.

Preoccupation intensified about who I am
And where I am,
Only to be censored by disillusionment.
A new day dawned though.

I am now in the shadows.
Here I am, involuntarily silent.
Here I can only observe
And be reminded of how it was.

I had many opportunities.
How much better it would have been
To leave imprints rather than missteps.
No legacy.

At best I lived and left only regrets.
Sadly, this brought untimely death.
If only I had the heart
To be what I could've been.

Intro: He Saw My Heart

I was different from the beginning. What can I say? I realized this particularly when my mom left for the United States, when I was seven. My dad whom I have seen a handful of times was definitely not around. His absence contributed to me being different.

However, being different was first felt when I started living with relatives, such as uncles, aunts, and cousins who had parents. This gave them a sense of connection and belonging. I on the other hand felt like I belonged to no one.

The feeling of not belonging was reinforced when I was boarded out with some friends of my Mom. I felt like the "odd" one out and needed to be maintained "somewhere" else. By the way, this is so cultural!!

This difference was also felt in school, especially when I saw the involvement of other parents with their children. I felt a deep sense of inadequacy, loss and resentment. Feelings of jealousy and doubt developed out of those confusing and unexplained time of life.

As a consequence, I became a girl and adult woman who constantly compared herself to others. I truly had difficulty celebrating the success of other women. My personality was ingrained with insecurities and unbelief. This difference needed to be understood. I needed inner work. Do you know anyone like that?

*Being confident of this that He who began a good work in you
will carry it on to completion until the day of Christ Jesus!*

— Philippians 1:6 —

Prompt: What truth have you kept buried that you need to unearth and be freed from?

He Saw My Heart And Saw The Truth

He saw my heart
And saw the truth, I wandered.
Did I enter to squander and plunder?

Oh! What evil betide?
Why the ache inside?
He saw my heart and saw the truth.

I created warm images in my mind
Of what love looked like.
Still, no peace resides.

He saw my heart and saw the truth.
It was a long goose chase.
What seemed the answer became disaster.

My character almost flawed.
That's all I have known,
To be seen and not heard

Who was I?
Who am I?
What am I?

Seldom was I asked how do you feel?
How do you know?
Are you cold inside?

Turmoil and self-doubt ensued!
A teen mom, a teen bride.
I was crushed—honestly.

I did not know I could be revived.
He saw my heart and saw the truth.
I no longer have to hide.

I can lift my head with grace and pride.
So, go on, go on!
Keep making strides.

Though at times I may make a blunder
He's had me covered
In the valleys and on the mountain side.

`He is the well-spring
That never runs dry!
He saw my heart and saw the truth!

Intro: My Freedom

After meditating on this particular day, I decided to bake a cake, using a recipe from a cooking channel. The same day, I replaced my skincare product and bought a red lipstick. I was feeling my own power— finally.

When you have heard for a long time, "If you wear make-up and lipstick you will go to hell." Or, "If you wear pants you will go to hell." Or "Gal nobody nah go want you. You haffi learn how fi cook. You won't get no good husband." (Translation: Girl nobody will want you, if you do not learn how to cook).

To this day, I do not enjoy cooking much, as I'm usually uncertain about myself in the kitchen. I still have to consciously guard my mind against the old narratives, allowed to take root in my mind, others had planted. I still don't wear make-up per se. Well, now I just use what I like – lip gloss mostly and the red lipstick to challenge my old way of thinking! I have now learned and understood that there is no correlation with "hell" and "make-up."

However, for a long time this ill-conceived mindset contributed to the creation of a persona which really wasn't me. For example, at times I pretended to be able to cook authentic Jamaican meals, only to be embarrassed.

I literally held my nose up at others, while yearning to be able to explore other interests and ideas. Inside, I was caving in, plagued with secretly trying to measure up to others who were receiving praise and attention for their success. Making matters worse, I ignored my abilities, talents and passions. This became exhausting! Plato said it best: "The first and best victory is to conquer self. To be conquered by self is of all things, the most shameful and vile." I am still trying to conquer self – the best and sweetest victory of all.

For we dare not make ourselves of the number or compare
ourselves with some that commend themselves;
but they measuring themselves by themselves and
comparing themselves among themselves are not wise.

— 2 Cor. 10:12 —

Prompt: What are you still fearing?

My Freedom

Learning to be free.
Seeing in my mind's eye freedom;
Recognizing the power therein
And boundless opportunities to win.

Learning to be free.
Christ has so much more for me.
The world denied and mocked Him.
Yet even in death He set captives free.

Learning to be free
Means doing the ordinary and mundane,
With simplicity and creativity,
Knowing His grace has set me free.

Learning to be free.
So, go ahead and wear that red lipstick.
See yourself where you want to be,
Knowing the Creator anchors me.

Go where you've never been,
Risk the unforbidden thing.
Accept self and embrace imagination.
I'm off the reservation. Yes! I'm free.

Formula
For Overcoming Unbelief And Fear

Establish Early Bed Time And Rising Time

Upon rising, do the following:

1 **Read your Bible & Pray (The Psalms for the Gospels) Or (Read poetry or other positive words)**

2 Say out loud your affirmations/Goal/Purpose in life **(Emotionalize this with music that is calming and filled with faith)**

3 Meditate for 30 minutes without interruptions (Link: *https://youtu. be/tEmt1Znux58*)
   *****If you have time journal or write down how you feel or any clarity you received during meditation/quiet time*****

Mid-Morning Practice: (Around 10 A.M.)

Reaffirm Yourself:

1 Find a quiet place.

2 Repeat your affirmations 5x's. (Remember to emotionalize your affirmations)

3 Check email and your social media *ONLY* **Mid-morning (dedicate time limit for this for this activity to reduce unproductive time)**

Mid-Afternoon (Around 3 P.M.)

Meditate & Empty Your Mind:

1   Find a quiet place and empty your mind

2   Visualize or imagine a quiet place you have been or your favorite spot in nature

3   Do 3-4 rounds of deep breathing, then relax your breathing to normal and focus on this tranquil place for 15 minutes **(Here is a link for examples on deep breathing: https://www.youtube.com/watch?v=K353fkHYMPs)**

4   Repeat your affirmations 5x's or read something positive for 10 minutes **(a book or something you've selected ahead of time)**

5   Check email and your social media *ONLY* **mid-afternoon (dedicate time limit for this activity to reduce unproductive time)**

Before Bed Practice: Prayer, Reflection, And Gratitude (Early to Bed)

1   Pray and give Thanks/Gratitude for the day regardless of how it turned out or what happened.

2   Write what you are thankful for and what you are proud of; or what you were able to accomplish. **(Keeping in mind that you are working toward your goals daily/weekly/monthly.)**

3   Make your "MISSION LIST" for the next day with your goal in mind.

4   REPEAT YOUR AFFIRMATIONS/GOALS (emotionalized with music).

5   Go to bed.

********YOU DID IT********

About The Author

Keisha Henry, MSW, LCSW, EMDR Psychotherapist

Keisha Henry, MSW, LCSW, is a trauma trained therapist working with women, adolescents, and parents (parent-education groups) for the past 16 years. Keisha completed her graduate degree in Clinical Social Work at Barry University, Miami Shores, Florida.

Keisha believes in a person-centered approach! Recognizing that the "whole-person" matters bring relevance to other aspects of a person's life that affects one's overall well-being. In her work, she finds that clients value this approach as one that preserves integrity, builds trust, understanding, and empowerment.

A native of Jamaica, West Indies, Keisha is a mother, wife, psychotherapist, and author. Keisha values the love, respect, and commitment of her husband and children as well as her practice and church community. In her spare time, Keisha enjoys spending time swimming, getting a workout in at the gym, and knitting.

Keisha is available for seminars, keynotes, and speaking engagements based upon her book *Healing of The Heart: Lessons From My Journey*.

She can be reached at 561-319-8055
or *K.henry@nbhi-llc.net*